BEGINNER'S GUIDE TO
Woodwork

Tony Lawler

Illustrated by Diana McLean

Designed by Graham Round
and Pica Design

Edited by Lisa Watts

Contents

First published in 1979, in a smaller format, under the title *Beginner's Guide to Woodwork*. This edition first published in 1988 by Usborne Publishing Ltd, 20 Garrick Street, London WC2E 9BJ, England.

Copyright © 1979, 1988 Usborne Publishing.

Printed in Britain.

How to use this book

This book is a basic guide to woodwork for beginners of all ages. Step-by-step pictures and instructions show you how to use woodworking tools and do the basic woodwork techniques. Then there are lots of things you can make to try out your woodworking skills.

If you want to find out how to do a particular woodworking job, look it up in the index or the list of contents. Then turn to the page and follow the pictures and instructions as you work with your tools.

The projects at the beginning of the book are easier than those further on, so work your way through and tackle the later ones as you get more experienced.

Look out for the pictures marked with a red star. These are the stages when you have to be especially careful — mistakes made here are hard to correct and can lead to disappointing results.

You do not need many tools to start off with — there are things you can make with just a saw, a hammer and nails. If you do want to buy tools, look at the guide at the back of the book. This shows what different tools are for and which are the most useful.

Remember, some woodworking tools are very sharp and can be dangerous. Always clamp your work and follow the instructions for using the tools carefully. There is a first aid section at the back of the book just in case you do have an accident.

When you have mastered the basic skills, you will probably want to work out your own projects. Then you can use this book to check how to do a technique, or look up a special term.

3

A place to work

You need to find somewhere to do your woodwork, where you can leave your tools and not worry about making too much mess. You also need a good, firm surface to work on.

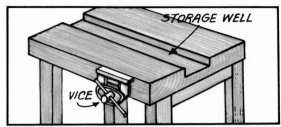

This is a specially designed woodworker's bench. It has a vice for clamping wood, a storage well for tools and a tough, smooth working surface.

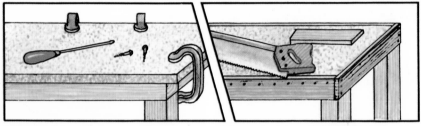

You could work at an ordinary table with a board clamped to the top to protect it.

A board with a rim glued and nailed to the edge fits over a table without needing clamps.

Some woodworkers keep their tools in a wooden box and use the top as a work surface.

You could look for an old crate to use as a work box, or try making yourself a wooden box*.

Looking after your tools

Find a place to keep your tools—a box, a bag, a drawer or an old crate. Always clean them before putting them away and make sure they are free from rust.

*See page 48 for how to make a box.

Working safely

A vice or some "G" clamps are essential tools for holding wood steady while you work. If the wood slips while you are sawing, chiselling or drilling, you will probably ruin your work and may hurt yourself. Holding the wood securely in a clamp also leaves both hands free to work with.

Never cut wood without resting it on something. If you do you are sure to have an accident.

Vices and clamps

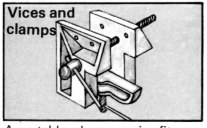

A portable, clamp-on vice fits on to most benches or tables. The screw at the front tightens to grip the wood.

SCRAP WOOD

Put pieces of scrap wood under "G" clamps so they do not mark your wood.

Using a sawing-board

A good way to support wood while you saw is by pushing it firmly against something. A sawing-board is useful for this. You can find out how to make one on page 17.

RIDGE

You hook the sawing-board over the edge of a table and push the wood firmly against the ridge on the sawing-board.

Instead of a sawing-board you could nail or clamp a block of wood to the work surface and push your wood against it.

Get as much help as you can by clamping and steadying your wood—especially for difficult or fiddly jobs. Remember, if the wood can wobble, you could have an accident.

More about vices, clamps and sawing-boards on page 51.   5

Wood and board

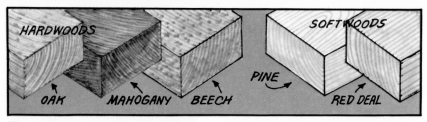

The colour, texture and strength of wood varies according to the type of tree it comes from. Hardwoods come from deciduous trees and softwoods come from coniferous trees. Generally, softwoods are cheaper and easier to work than hardwoods.

Wood consists of tight bundles of fibres. The way the fibres are arranged give the wood its pattern called the grain.

Always be careful when you are working along the grain of the wood as this is where it may split.

Man-made boards

These are various types of board which are made from wood, but are cheaper and less likely to split than natural wood.

Thin sheets of wood which are bonded together with glue. The grain runs in opposite directions in each sheet.

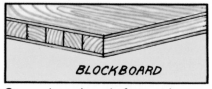

Strong board made from strips of wood sandwiched between two thin sheets of wood.

Thin board made from wood dust mixed with resins then pressed into sheets. It is cheap but not very strong.

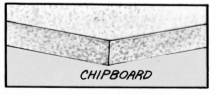

Strong, cheap but heavy board made from chips of wood mixed with resins and then compressed.

More about wood on page 59.

Buying wood

A piece of wood has three measurements: width, thickness and length. When you buy wood you need to tell the shop assistant all of these measurements.

In this book the measurements are in millimetres (mm). The width is always given first, then the thickness, then the length.

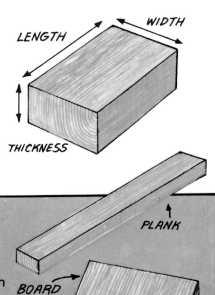

Planks and boards

Planks are made in standard widths and thicknesses. They are always a bit smaller than their standard measurements because they are planed smooth after being cut to size.

Man-made boards are made in various thicknesses and you buy a piece the width and length you want.

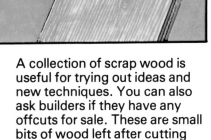

Wood for free

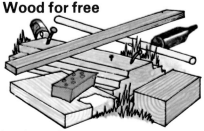

Look out for wood in rubbish dumps or tips and collect pieces good enough to use.

A collection of scrap wood is useful for trying out ideas and new techniques. You can also ask builders if they have any offcuts for sale. These are small bits of wood left after cutting the wood for a job.

Clean up wood when you find it and cut it to manageable shapes. Never use rotten or wormy wood.

PULL OUT NAILS

SCRAPE OFF PAINT

CUT TO SIZE

For reshaping old wood, see page 20.

Basic tools

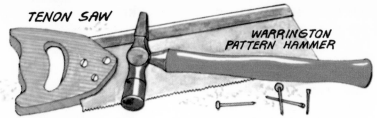

TENON SAW

WARRINGTON PATTERN HAMMER

For your first woodwork projects all you need is a saw and a hammer. It does not matter if your tools are not quite like those in the picture. Before you start a job, always check your tools—make sure the hammer head and saw handle are secure.

How to saw

Stand comfortably with the wood on a sawing-board, or clamped. Start off with a light backward stroke to make a line.

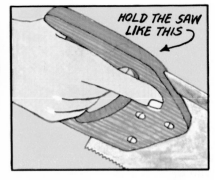

HOLD THE SAW LIKE THIS

Nails and nailing

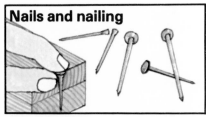

Nails should reach over half-way through both pieces of wood. They should never go through to the other side.

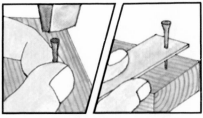

Start nails off with the thin side of the hammer head, or push the nail through a piece of card to support it.

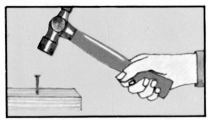

Grip the hammer lightly at the end of the handle and watch the head of the nail while you hammer.

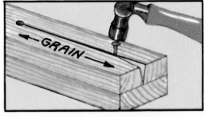

GRAIN

If you put two nails along the same line of grain, the wood will probably split, so stagger the nails along the wood.

Measuring

Before you start a job, you need to mark all the measurements on the wood. It is very important to measure accurately — even 0.5mm can be critical and mean that the pieces will not fit together. If you make mistakes marking out, there is very little you can do about them later.

Marking out tools

TRY SQUARE   SHARP PENCIL
METAL RULE

A try square is for drawing lines across the wood at right-angles to the sides.

Mark the length you want, then put the try square on the mark and draw a line across the wood.

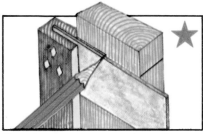

Use the try square to draw the line all round the wood.

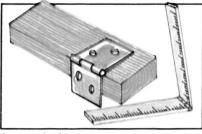

Instead of a try square you could use a large hinge or a folding ruler.

As you mark out the wood, shade in the areas you are not going to use.

Cutting to size

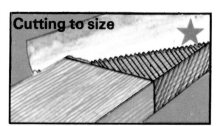

To saw a piece of wood exactly to size, always cut on the outside, or waste side, of the line.

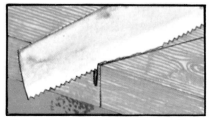

This is because about 3mm of wood are lost as sawdust. If you do not allow for this your sizes will not be accurate.

9

Joining wood

One of the simplest ways to join wood is with nails. You should always glue the surfaces together as well, though, to make a strong joint. It is important to use the right glue — woodworking adhesive, also called PVA glue, is best. For most jobs, use small nails called panel pins.

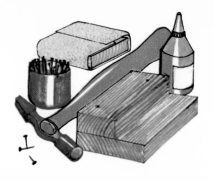

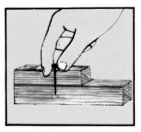

Pins should go over half-way through both pieces of wood.

Hammer the pins half-way into one of the pieces of wood.

Spread glue on the other piece of wood.

Removing glue

If you get any PVA glue on yourself or your clothes, wash it off straight away with water. Glue that has dried is very difficult to remove.

Put the pieces together and hammer the pins in.

Leave for at least two hours for the glue to set.

KNOCK THE NAILS DOWN LIKE THIS

For a neat finish, use a blunt nail, or a nail punch, to hammer the pins below the surface.

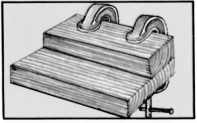

You can glue the joint without using nails if you want. Clamp the wood while the glue sets.

Some boats to make

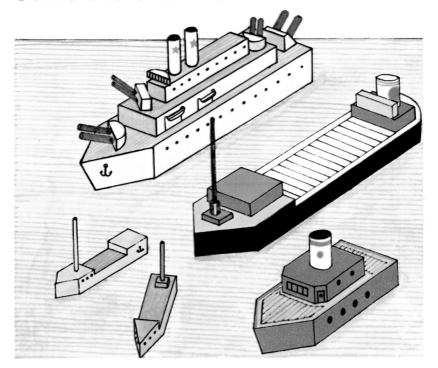

What you need

Model boats like these can be made from scraps or offcuts of wood. No measurements are given so you can plan and design boats to fit your wood.

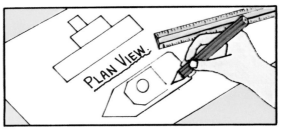

First, design and draw a boat on paper. Draw it side view and from above (plan view), then work out the measurements.

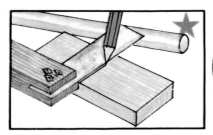

Mark the measurements on the wood, then saw it, cutting on the waste side of the lines.

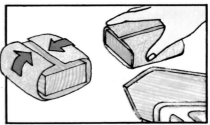

Wrap a piece of glasspaper* round a block of wood and smooth the edges and surfaces.

*Glasspaper, also called sandpaper, see page 18.

11

Then try the pieces together to make sure they fit.

Hammer panel pins into the top piece first.

Then glue the pieces and hammer the pins right in.

Glue on funnels and other parts and clamp for two hours.

Hammer the pin heads down with a blunt nail.

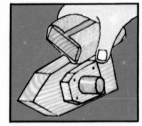

Smooth the boat with fine glasspaper before painting.

Ideas for painting

To finish the boat, paint in the deckboards, portholes, and other details. You can use watercolour or poster paints, or enamel paints from a modelling shop. If you use watercolour paint, give the boats a coat of clear varnish—either brush-on or aerosol—when the paint is dry.

More things to make

Screws and drilling

Screws are a stronger and better way of fixing wood than nails. There are lots of different shapes and sizes of screws. These are described in more detail on page 53.

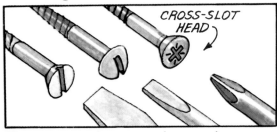

CROSS-SLOT HEAD

Choose screws long enough to reach over half-way through both pieces of wood. Always use a screwdriver that fits the screws.

GIMLET

Make holes (called pilot holes) with a gimlet or drill.

Then screw the screws into the pilot holes. Push firmly on the screwdriver as you turn it in a clockwise direction.

Hand drilling

HOLD DRILL UPRIGHT

SIZE MARKED ON DRILL IS SIZE HOLE IT MAKES

Clamp the wood with a piece of scrap wood under it when you drill.

STICKY TAPE

Mark the depth to be drilled with a piece of sticky tape.

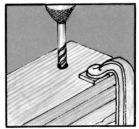

For matching holes, clamp two pieces of wood together.

Holes for screws

SHANK

THREAD

COUNTERSINK BIT

You need to drill two holes—one the size of the shank and one the size of the thread. Make a shallow hole for the head of the screw with a countersink bit.

More about screws on page 53 and drills on page 56.

Swing-lid box

If you mark out the measurements for this box accurately, it should fit together with no problems.

What you need

You could use softwood such as pine for the sides and ends, and plywood for the lid and base. Use panel pins and PVA glue to assemble the box and a screw for the lid.

Sides: 2 pieces 50mm × 12mm × 250mm
Ends: 2 pieces 50mm × 25mm × 50mm
Lid and base: 2 pieces 120mm × 6mm × 250mm

(The width is given first, then the thickness, then the length.)

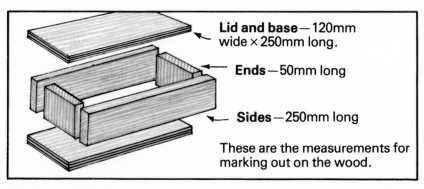

Lid and base — 120mm wide × 250mm long.

Ends — 50mm long

Sides — 250mm long

These are the measurements for marking out on the wood.

Mark the measurements with a ruler and use a try square to get your lines at right-angles to the sides.

Cut the wood, sawing on the waste side of the lines.

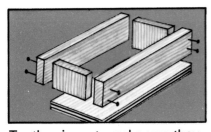

UNCUT EDGES NEXT TO SIDES

Try the pieces to make sure they fit and glasspaper if necessary. Hammer the panel pins half-way into the wood.

Apply the glue and hammer the box together. Use a vice or clamps to hold it steady.

Fitting the lid

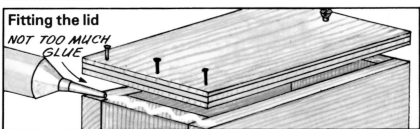

NOT TOO MUCH GLUE

Position the lid so it overlaps the box at the sides, then glue and nail one end to the box.

Drill a pilot hole at the other end and screw the lid to the box. Do not glue this end.

With the box firmly clamped, saw through the lid at an angle, like this. Then saw off the overlapping edges of the lid and base.

Painting the box

Before painting or varnishing the box, smooth it all over with glasspaper. You can paint it with gloss paint, or watercolour with a coat of varnish on top.

15

Another way to join wood

Dowels are machine-made rods of hardwood which can be used like nails to join pieces of wood. They are glued into the wood and give a neater finish than nails. Dowels are made in various diameters and you buy a piece the size and length you need.

You can buy smooth or grooved dowels. If you get smooth ones, you have to saw a shallow groove in them yourself.

Saw the groove with the dowel firmly clamped. Dowels without a groove would split the wood when they are hammered in.

The dowel should be fitted into a hole exactly the same size as itself, so choose a drill bit of the correct size.

Put a piece of tape on the drill to mark the depth for a hole over half-way through both pieces of wood.

Clamp the two pieces of wood together and drill the holes. Stop when the tape reaches the wood.

Put glue on the dowels and tap them into the holes. Listen for the change in note when they reach the bottom.

Carefully saw off the tops of the dowels, then glasspaper the stumps till they are flush with the wood.

How to make a sawing-board

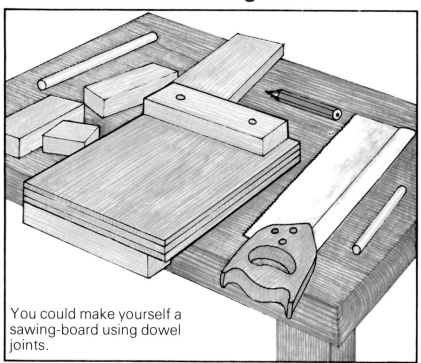

You could make yourself a
sawing-board using dowel
joints.

What you need

The sawing-board
needs to be sturdy, so
use hardwood such as
beech, for the end
pieces. The centre
piece could be
plywood. The
dimensions shown on
the right make a useful
sized sawing-board.

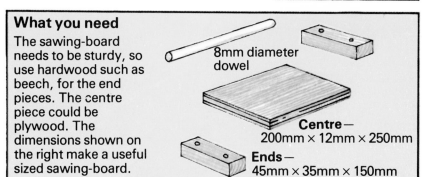

8mm diameter
dowel

Centre—
200mm × 12mm × 250mm

Ends—
45mm × 35mm × 150mm

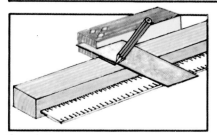

Carefully mark out the
measurements on the wood.

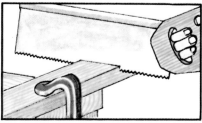

Saw the materials to size cutting
on the waste side of the lines.

Fixing the end pieces

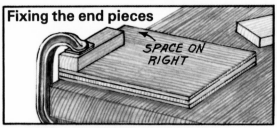

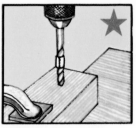

Clamp one end piece in position with a space on the right if you are right-handed or on the left if you are left-handed.

With an 8mm drill, make the holes for the dowels.

Saw grooves in the dowels, then apply the glue and tap them into the holes.

Saw off the dowels and smooth the tops with glasspaper. Fix the other end piece to the board in the same way.

Glasspaper

This is the proper name for what is sometimes called sandpaper. It is made in different grades of roughness, and is used mainly for smoothing wood after it has been sawn, filed or planed. The finer papers give a smoother finish than the rougher grades.

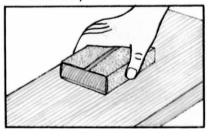

Use glasspaper wrapped round a block of scrap wood so you get an even pressure as you rub.

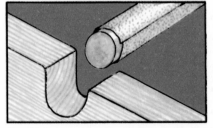

Always rub along the grain of the wood, with a rough paper first, then a finer one.

For holes or round edges you can wrap glasspaper round a piece of dowel.

How to use a plane

A plane has a sharp blade which cuts long slivers from the wood. It is useful for giving wood a smooth surface and for shaving it down to precise measurements. For sharpening plane blades see page 58.

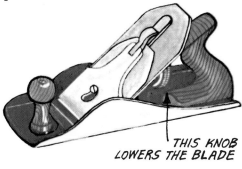

THIS KNOB
LOWERS THE BLADE

GRAIN

Always plane the wood in the same direction as the grain.

GRAIN

If you plane against the grain it cuts off jagged chips.

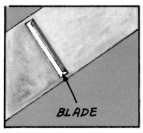

BLADE

When you lower the blade the plane cuts thicker shavings.

Make a small test stroke to find which way the grain runs, then clamp the wood and start planing from one end.

STOP BEFORE YOU REACH THE END

Keep the same downwards pressure as you push the plane to the other end. Check the surface after each stroke.

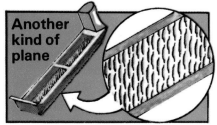

Another kind of plane

A shaper plane can be used instead of an ordinary plane. It is cheaper but does not make such a smooth surface.

Use a shaper plane in the same way as an ordinary plane, making long, smooth strokes.

More about planes and shaper planes on page 55.

19

Reshaping old wood

With a plane or shaper plane you can accurately smooth timber down to new dimensions. This is very useful for renovating old wood. It is a tricky process and it needs care and practice to get the sides of the wood at right-angles to each other.

First mark out the timber larger than the final sizes you want, to make it a manageable shape.

Cut the wood, sawing on the waste side of the lines.

Then clamp it securely and plane one side to make it absolutely flat.

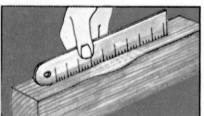

Check for flatness by holding a metal rule on the wood. If a chink of light shows through, the surface is uneven.

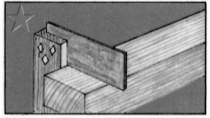

Plane the next side flat. Aim to get it at right-angles to the first and keep checking it with a try square.

Plane all the sides flat and at right-angles to each other.

Then mark out the final sizes you want on the wood and very carefully plane it down to these lines.

Files and rasps

These are for smoothing and shaping wood. They vary in roughness, shape and size, the different types being suited to different jobs.

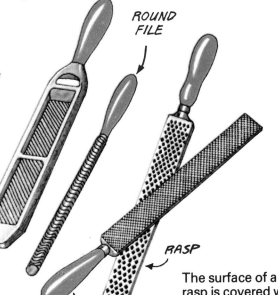

ROUND FILE

A shaper file has tiny teeth which grate away little chips of wood.

SHAPER FILE

Files have a ridged surface. They are for finer work than shaper files or rasps.

FLAT FILE

RASP

The surface of a rasp is covered with sharp knobs. Clean rasps and files with a wire brush when they clog up.

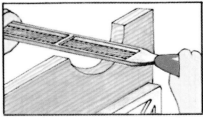

Grip a file or rasp in both hands and pull it backwards and forwards across the wood. It cuts only on the forward stroke.

Use a rasp at an angle across the wood so it does not tear the fibres.

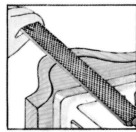

Files are for shaping and smoothing wood after sawing.

For flat surfaces use a plane rather than a file or rasp as these tend to round off the edges.

More about files, rasps and shaper tools on pages 54-55.

Sawing shapes

Saws like this are for cutting curves and shapes in wood. You need lots of blades as they are very thin and often break.

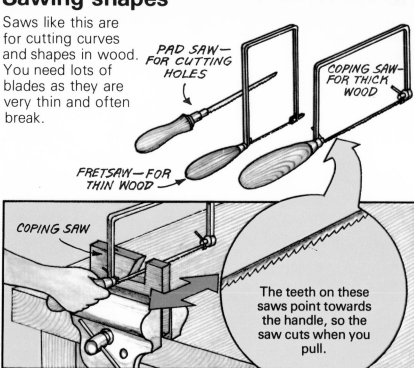

PAD SAW—FOR CUTTING HOLES

COPING SAW—FOR THICK WOOD

FRETSAW—FOR THIN WOOD

COPING SAW

The teeth on these saws point towards the handle, so the saw cuts when you pull.

How to saw

Clamp the wood, then start sawing, turning the handle as you saw so that the blade follows the line. This is quite tricky so saw a little outside the line and smooth the wood down with glasspaper, or a fine file, afterwards. If the blade breaks, undo the screws and put in a new one.

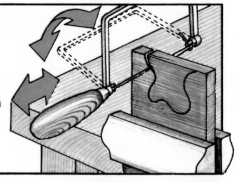

Fretsawing

CUT THIS SHAPE WITH A COPING SAW

A board like this is useful for supporting thin wood which shakes and may split when you fretsaw it.

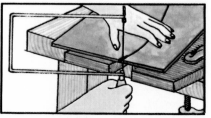

Clamp the edge of the board to the table. Hold the thin wood on top and move it so the saw follows the line.

Wooden animals to make

To make wooden animals like these, cut the shapes from pine or plywood with a coping saw.

PLYWOOD EARS GLUED ON

Draw the animal on a piece of paper and glue it to the wood.

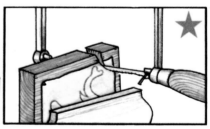

Clamp the wood firmly and saw round the shape, keeping outside the line.

Be careful
Watch the grain of the wood as you saw. Be very careful sawing along the grain as this is where the wood may split. Smooth the shape with a file or glasspaper.

THE WOOD MAY SPLIT HERE

GRAIN

Glue on any bits that break off. Do not glasspaper them.

How to make a bagatelle game

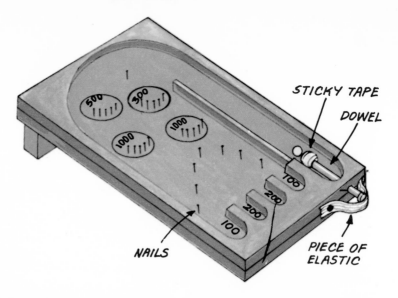

STICKY TAPE

DOWEL

NAILS

PIECE OF ELASTIC

This is made from two pieces of board. Cut the shape for the game from one of the boards with a coping saw.

Glue and nail the boards together and drill the hole for the trigger. Smooth with glasspaper and varnish or paint with gloss paint.

How to make a book-rack

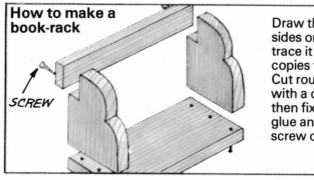

SCREW

Draw the shape for the sides on paper. Then trace it and glue both copies to the wood. Cut round the shapes with a coping saw, then fix the base with glue and nails and screw on the back rail.

Kangaroo

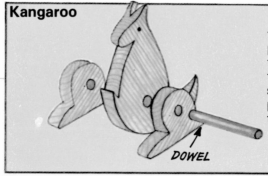

DOWEL

Draw the shapes for the body and legs on paper and glue them to the wood. Saw round them with a coping saw, then clamp the pieces together and drill the hole for the dowel.

How to chisel

Chisels are used mainly for cutting joints in wood. A good chisel is very sharp, so always clamp the wood and work with the chisel pointing away from you — and other people.

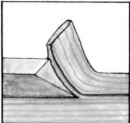

A chisel cuts by slicing between the fibres of the wood.

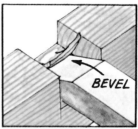

The slope on one side of the chisel blade is called the bevel.

You must make a saw-cut each side of the section before you chisel it out.

If you chisel deeper than the saw-cuts the wood will probably split.

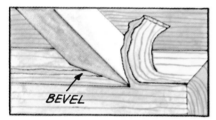

To dig out chips of wood, hold the chisel with the bevel at the bottom.

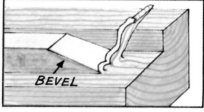

With the bevel at the top, you can smooth off the surface of the wood. Hold the chisel flat so that it does not dig in.

To help you chisel, use a mallet. A hammer would split the handle of the chisel. If you do not have a mallet, use a block of wood, or wrap a cloth round your hammer.

More about chisels on p. 54. For sharpening chisels see p.58.

Joints without nails

By carefully cutting sections from wood you can fit them together without nails or screws.

When you make these joints, be very careful marking them out. If they turn out too big there is little you can do to correct them. It is a good idea to try some out on scrap wood first.

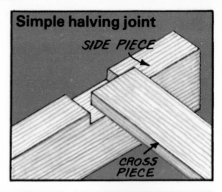

Simple halving joint

SIDE PIECE

CROSS PIECE

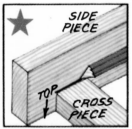

Mark the thickness of the cross piece on the side piece.

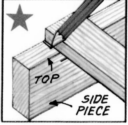

Then mark the width of the cross piece on the side piece.

Check the lines and shade the wood to be cut out.

Make saw cuts just inside each end of the shaded section.

With the bevel at the bottom, chisel out chips of wood.

Turn the wood round and chisel from the other side.

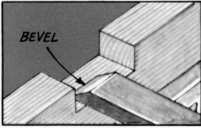

Then clean up the base of the joint by using the chisel with the bevel at the top.

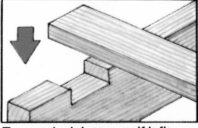

Try out the joint to see if it fits, but do not squeeze or hammer it in.

If the joint is too big you could try filling it with woodfiller.

If it is too small, plane one side of the cross piece.

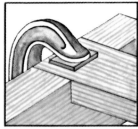

Finally, glue the joint and clamp it till it dries.

Other woodwork joints

HOUSING JOINT

STOPPED HOUSING JOINT

CROSS-HALVING JOINT

These joints are made using the same techniques as for the simple halving joint. Remember to be especially careful marking them out and to saw on the waste side of the lines.

How to make stilts

You need two long pieces of wood about 40mm wide and 25mm thick, two blocks 40mm × 60mm × 150mm and some 50mm long screws.

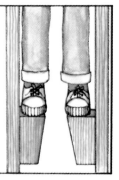

Mark the position for the blocks about 300mm up the sticks.

SAW THIS OFF

Saw the blocks to this shape and glasspaper.

Drill pilot holes and glue and screw the blocks to the sticks.

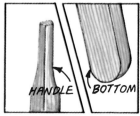

HANDLE BOTTOM

Shape the handles and round off the bottom of the sticks.

Go-kart and sledge

The body of this go-kart is a sledge which you can unbolt and use in the snow.

Sledge

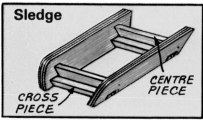

Make the sides of the sledge from plywood and use 75mm × 25mm × 350mm wood for the cross and centre pieces.

Clamp two pieces of plywood together and mark the shape for the sides and the slots for the cross pieces.

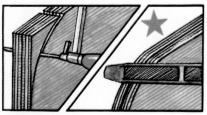

Saw round the sides and smooth them down, then chisel out the slots.

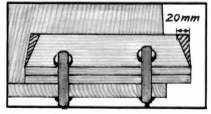

Clamp the centre pieces together and saw off the ends at an angle. This gives the sledge sloping sides and makes it stable.

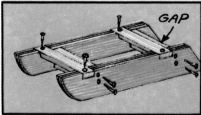

Glue and screw the cross and centre pieces in position. Leave 20mm between them at the back for the go-kart backrest.

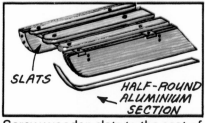

Screw wooden slats to the seat of the sledge and strips of half-round aluminium section to the runners.

Go-kart

To convert the sledge to a go-kart you need a set of old pram wheels, some wood 75mm wide and 50mm thick and coach bolts 100mm long and 8mm in diameter.

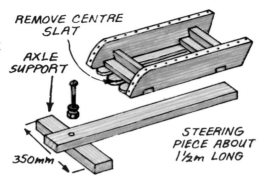

REMOVE CENTRE SLAT

AXLE SUPPORT

STEERING PIECE ABOUT 1½m LONG

350mm

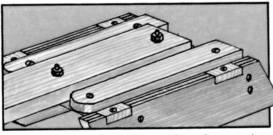

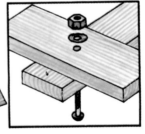

Drill holes, then bolt the steering piece to the sledge. Leave a space at the back for fitting the back axle.

Bolt the axle support to the front of the steering piece.

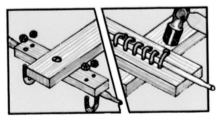

NAILS OR LONG "U" BOLTS

Fix the front axle to the axle support with "U" bolts or nails hammered over.

Bolt or nail the back axle to the back of the sledge and fit the wheels on the axles.

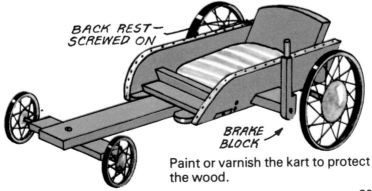

BACK REST — SCREWED ON

BRAKE BLOCK

Paint or varnish the kart to protect the wood.

Protecting wood

Wood is porous and unless you protect it with varnish, paint or some other kind of finish, it absorbs moisture and becomes dirty. Here are some of the finishes you can use.

PAINTED TOYS

VARNISHED NESTING BOX

The sort of finish you choose depends on what the object is to be used for, so bear this in mind before you decide.

Wax polishing

This gives wood a smooth, shiny surface and looks good on furniture. It stops fingerprints and dust dirtying the wood, but water will stain it.

GRAIN

Rub the wax into the grain with a rough cloth.

Polish it with a soft cloth, rubbing along the grain.

Varnish

This can be either glossy or matt and gives a tough, waterproof finish. There are lots of different kinds of varnish, so ask the shop assistant which you should buy.

Read the instructions to find out how to apply your varnish—some are brushed on, some put on with a cloth and some are sprayed.

Outdoor finishes

For outdoors you need to give the wood a hardwearing, waterproof surface or it will warp and rot. Paint, varnish and creosote are all suitable.

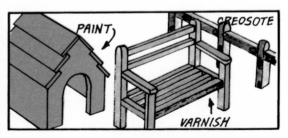

PAINT

CREOSOTE

VARNISH

Do not use creosote on seats as it stains clothes. It also gives off vapours which are harmful for pets.

Preparing the wood

Before you paint, varnish or wax the wood you have to make the surface absolutely smooth and put a seal on the wood. Sealing is explained on the next page.

You need to plane the sawn edges of the wood to make them smooth. Remember to plane in the direction of the grain.

Glasspaper all the surfaces, using a coarse paper first, then a fine one.

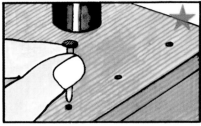

Knock the heads of any nails into the wood with a blunt nail or a nail punch.

Woodfiller

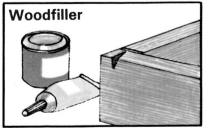

Next, fill any cracks and nail holes with woodfiller. You can buy this in colours to match your wood.

Instead of woodfiller you can mix PVA glue with sawdust to make a thick paste. Try it out on scrap wood first.

Push the woodfiller well into the cracks and holes, then smooth with a scraper or old knife.

After about an hour, when the woodfiller is dry, glasspaper the surface to make it smooth.

Sealing the wood

The seal forms a smooth coating on the surface of the wood. It stops the paint, wax or varnish sinking into the grain. Always apply the right kind of seal for the finish you are using.

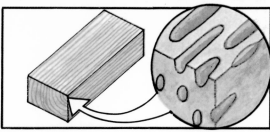

The seal fills up the tiny pits and tubes between the fibres on the surface of the wood.

Which seal to use

If you are going to varnish or wax the wood, you can seal it with varnish thinned with turpentine. Use two parts of varnish to one part of turpentine.

For paint, seal the wood with a paint undercoat.

Do not use any seal with creosote as it is supposed to sink right into the wood.

Apply two coats of seal to get a really smooth surface. Let the first coat dry and glasspaper it before applying the second.

Painting and varnishing

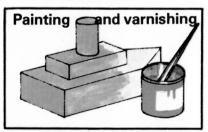

For best results, always apply at least two coats of paint or varnish.

Make sure the first coat is absolutely dry before you apply the second one.

Wood stains

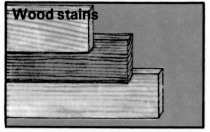

These come in various colours and can be used to stain wood to make it look like a hardwood.

Do not use a seal when you stain wood. Apply two coats of stain, then varnish on top.

Elastic band dragster

To make this dragster you need two thin pieces of wood for the sides and wheels, two small blocks to put between the sides and some dowel for the axles.

Nail the two thin pieces of wood together and draw the car and wheels on one side.

Saw out the shapes and glasspaper them. If the wheels are not round, put elastic bands on them, like tyres.

Drill holes the same size as the dowel for the axles.

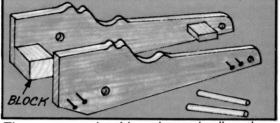

Then separate the sides, glue and nail on the blocks and fit the axles and wheels. Glue the back wheels to their axle.

Put a small nail in the front block and another in the rear axle and hook an elastic band round them.

To work the dragster, turn the back wheel to wind up the elastic band, then let go . . . .

How to make a rocking-horse

The rockers of this small rocking-horse are held in place by dowels. You could use the same technique to make a small stool or table.

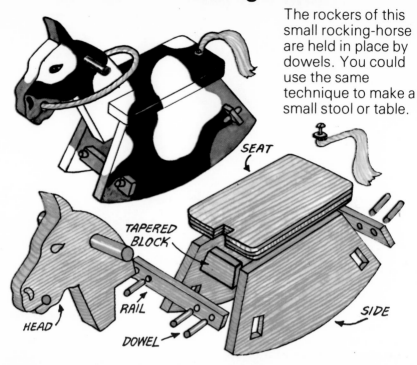

SEAT

TAPERED BLOCK

HEAD

RAIL

DOWEL

SIDE

What you need

Sides: 2 pieces of plywood 350mm × 10mm × 450mm.
Blocks: 2 pieces of wood or board 50mm × 25mm × 150mm.
Rails: 2 pieces of softwood 50mm × 25mm × 400mm.
Seat: 1 piece of plywood 250mm × 15mm × 500mm.
Head: 1 piece plywood 350mm × 15mm × 350mm.

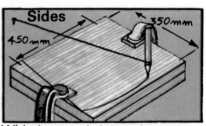

Sides

450mm   350mm

With the wood clamped together, mark out the measurements for the sides. Draw the curve with a piece of string 600mm long.

Saw the sides with the wood still clamped together.

KEEP CLOSE TO WOOD

Mark the positions for the rails by drawing round them.

HOLES TO PUT BLADE THROUGH

Saw out the holes for the rails with a coping saw.

Blocks

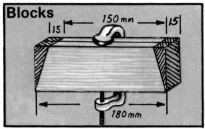

Clamp together the wood for the blocks and mark out the sizes shown here.

Saw the blocks to size, but do not glasspaper them as this would alter the shape.

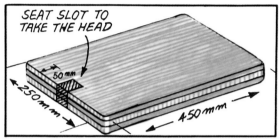

Mark out and saw the seat to the sizes shown above. The slot for the head should be just wide enough for the head to fit into.

Saw down the sides of the slot, then chisel it out.

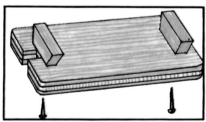

Drill pilot holes for the screws, then glue and screw the blocks to the seat.

Try the sides and rails in position (no glue yet) and carefully mark where the sides cross the rails.

Rails

Drill the holes for the dowels so that the edge of each hole is exactly on the line marking the width of the sides.

Taper off one end of the outside dowels with a file or chisel.

35

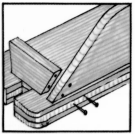

Drill pilot holes, then glue and screw the sides to the blocks.

Fit the rails and push the inside dowels into place.

Tap in the outside dowels. They must fit tightly.

Head

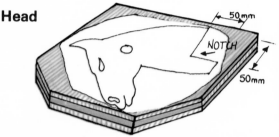

Draw the head shape on paper and glue it to the wood. Make sure you mark the notch at the back correctly.

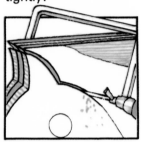

Saw round the head with a coping saw.

Drill then saw out a hole for the handle.

Fit the head by screwing and glueing it to the seat and block. Glue in the handle and plait some string for the tail.

Smooth all the surfaces and edges with fine glasspaper — make sure there are no splinters.

To paint the horse, use undercoat first, then two coats of gloss paint.

More ways to join wood

There are lots of different kinds of fittings that you can buy to make joints. These are called knockdown fittings because they can be easily dismantled if you want to take the wood apart again.

Shelf pegs

PEG
SOCKET

These are for supporting shelves. Drill holes for the sockets in the upright part of the shelves. Put the sockets in the holes and push the pegs into the sockets.

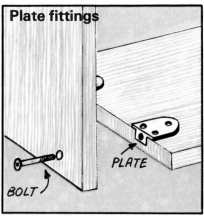

Plate fittings

PLATE
BOLT

Use these for joining boards. Mark the position for the plate and bolt, then drill a hole for the bolt and chisel out a bit of wood so the plate lies flat.

Block fittings

You could use block fittings for joining the sides of a cupboard. Each fitting consists of two small plastic blocks.

Screw the blocks to the board on either side of the joint. Push them together and do up the screws.

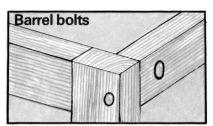

Barrel bolts

These are for joining the sections of a frame. A long bolt screws into a barrel in the opposite section.

BOLT
BARREL

Drill a hole for the bolt in both pieces of wood and a hole for the barrel. Test the joint before tightening the bolt.

Hinges

You have to be very careful positioning hinges. They are usually the last part of a project and mistakes can spoil the whole job.

There are lots of different kinds of hinges, so ask the shop assistant which you should use for your job. Butt hinges are the most common.

Butt hinges

These can be set into the wood or mounted on the outside if the wood is very thin.

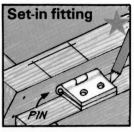

Set-in fitting

Mark round the hinge on the lid and base.

MARK THICKNESS ON LID AND BASE

Mark out half the thickness of the closed hinge.

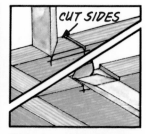

CUT SIDES

Chisel out the wood, cutting the sides with the chisel first.

Put the hinges in position. The centre of the pins should be level with the back of the wood.

Make pilot holes with a small drill or nail for one screw in each side of the hinge.

Screw the hinges in place with only one screw in each side, then try closing the lid.

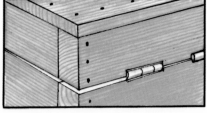

If the hinges are not in the right position, you can adjust them with the other screws.

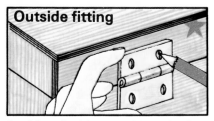

Outside fitting

Position the hinges with their pin level with the joint. Make pilot holes for one screw in each side of the hinges.

Put the first screws in, then check the fitting. If the screws are too long, file off the ends on the inside.

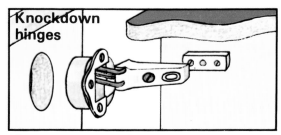

Knockdown hinges

These are designed for using on chipboard cupboards and are sold with instructions for fitting.

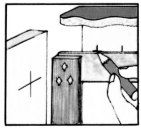

Carefully follow the instructions for marking out.

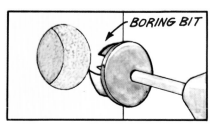

BORING BIT

Drill the large hole in the door with a special "boring bit" on a carpenter's brace or electric drill.

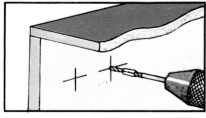

Drill pilot holes in the wall of the cupboard for the block part of the hinge and screw it on with screws for chipboard.

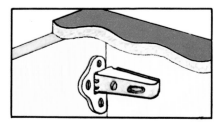

Slide the two halves of the hinge together and secure with the screws provided. Do not tighten the screws yet.

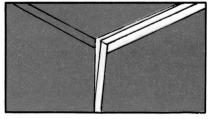

You can correct the way that the door hangs by adjusting the position of the fixing screw.

How to make a small table

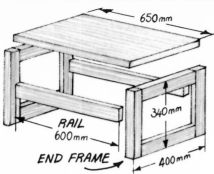

650mm
340mm
RAIL
600mm
END FRAME
400mm

This table has two end frames which are held apart by the side rails and the top. The dimensions given here make a small rectangular table. Use 50mm × 25mm wood for the frames and rails, and 6mm thick plywood or board for the top.

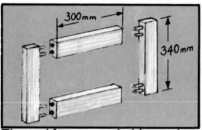

300mm
340mm

The end frames are held together with dowels which do not show when the pieces are assembled.

You have to be very careful positioning the holes so try out this technique on scrap wood*.

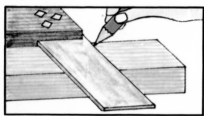

Mark out all the measurements on the wood, being careful to keep the ends square.

To cut the pieces of the frame the same length, clamp them together when you saw.

KEEP PENCIL CLOSE TO WOOD

Lay out the pieces for the frames and mark where they join.

SIDE PIECE
CROSS PIECE

Draw lines down the centre of the surfaces to be joined.

LEAVE NAILS STICKING OUT

Put nails in the cross pieces to mark where the dowels go.

*For another way to make these joints see page 43.

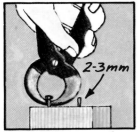

Clip off the tops of the nails with pincers or pliers.

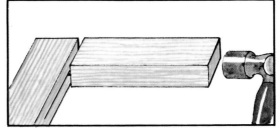

Then carefully tap the pieces together. The nails in the cross pieces will mark where the dowels should go in the side pieces.

Open the pieces up again and pull out the nails.

If the nails are hard to pull out, ease them up first.

Use dowels about 40mm long. Make grooves in them.

Choose a drill the same diameter as the dowels.

Drill the holes for the dowels exactly on the nail marks.

After drilling, try the pieces together without any glue.

If the holes are not in the right position you could shave the sides of the dowels, or use only one dowel per joint.

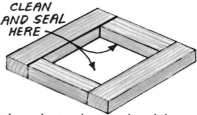

It is easier to clean and seal the inner surfaces of the frames before you glue them. Do not seal the surfaces to be glued.

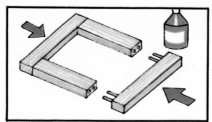

Next, glue the dowels and surfaces to be joined and fit the frames together.

You need to clamp the frames while the glue dries. For this you could use a sash cramp, or one of the ways shown below.

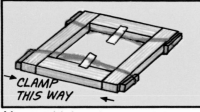

You could tie string round the frame, then tighten the string by twisting scraps of wood between the strands.

Another way is to nail wooden blocks to a board, then hammer wedges between the frame and the blocks.

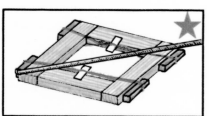

Before the glue dries make sure the diagonals are the same length and adjust if necessary.

Leave the frame under pressure for at least four hours, then if any pieces have slipped plane or file them flat.

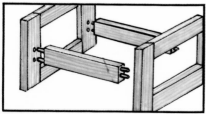

The rails are also held in place with secret dowel joints. Fit these in the same way as for the end frames.

Put nails in the rails and mark where the dowels should go in the frames.

Drill the holes for the dowels, then check that the pieces fit together before you glue them.

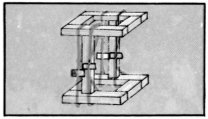

Use the string method to put pressure on the frame and leave it to dry for at least four hours.

Fitting the top

IRON-ON EDGE STRIP

If you want a plastic laminate table top, cut it larger than the top, glue it on with "Evo-Stik" then plane to size (see pp. 46-47).

Use metal angle pieces like these to fix the top to the table. Screw the angle pieces to the frame first.

Another method

If you find dowel joints difficult, glue the frames first.

Then drill the holes for the dowels.

Be careful the joints do not break as you hammer in the dowels.

Other ideas

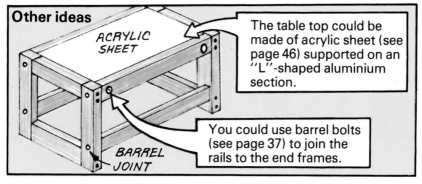

ACRYLIC SHEET

BARREL JOINT

The table top could be made of acrylic sheet (see page 46) supported on an "L"-shaped aluminium section.

You could use barrel bolts (see page 37) to join the rails to the end frames.

Planning a job

When you design your own woodwork projects you need to work out just what you want and how you are going to do it before you spend money on materials. When you work out your design, think of what it is to be used for and make sure your design and materials are suitable.

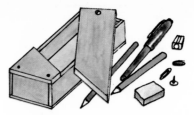

The design of even a simple project such as a pencil box depends on the size of the things to go in it.

If, say, you want to put up some shelves, you need to study the things to go on them before you work out your design.

ORNAMENTS AND PHOTOS

BOOKS

RECORDS AND RECORD PLAYER

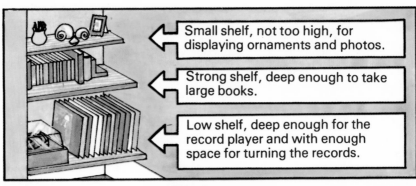

Small shelf, not too high, for displaying ornaments and photos.

Strong shelf, deep enough to take large books.

Low shelf, deep enough for the record player and with enough space for turning the records.

Draw a plan of the design you decide upon.

Choose a suitable method to support the shelves.

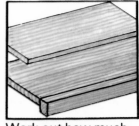

Work out how much and what sort of wood you need.

Making your own designs

To design a small table, decide what it is to be used for and where it will stand.

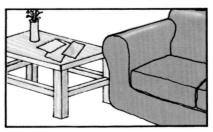

The table needs to be the right height for the furniture in the room.

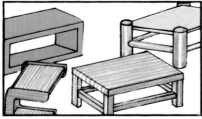

Choose the style of table you want. You can get ideas from shops, books or magazines.

Then make a card or balsa wood model of the design to find out if there are any problems.

Try out any new techniques on scrap wood before you finally decide on the design.

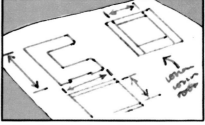

It is helpful to draw the design from three views—plan, side and front view.

When you buy the materials take a "cutting list" with drawings of the pieces.

Finally, work out which jobs to do first and write a "job list".

Working with other materials

When you plan your own woodwork jobs you may find there are other materials you want to use. Plastic laminate, such as "Formica" is useful for shelves and cupboards and you can use clear acrylic sheet, such as "Perspex" instead of glass. If you look round the shops there are lots of metal and plastic handles, edgings, drawer and door slides, and other fittings that you may find useful.

Plastic laminate

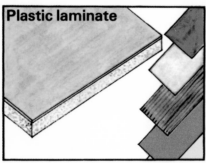
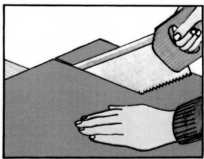

You can buy this as thin sheets, or ready-glued to a chipboard base. It also comes in strips for finishing edges and there are lots of different colours and textures.

Cut plastic laminate sheet with a saw and glue it to board with contact adhesive (see opposite). Always cut it larger than the board and plane the edges when it is stuck down.

Metals

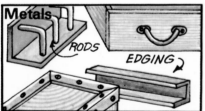

RODS

EDGING

You can buy handles, hinges and protective edgings made of steel, aluminium or brass. These metals can also be bought as sheets or rods.

Plastic

EDGE LIPPING

DOOR SLIDES

HANDLE

These are some of the plastic fittings you can buy. Look round in hardware shops to find just what you want.

Acrylic sheet

You can use clear or coloured acrylic sheet for cupboard doors and table tops. Cut and shape it with woodworking tools.

You can also bend and shape acrylic sheet by heating it in a warm oven. Wear gloves to pick up hot acrylic.

Which glue to use

PVA or woodworking adhesive is suitable for most kinds of wood, but when you use other materials you will need to use different kinds of glue.

PVA glue

You can use PVA glue for sticking porous materials such as wood, card, paper, fabric and felt.

Resin wood glue

"Cascamite" and other resin wood glues give a waterproof bond. Mix the glue with water according to the instructions.

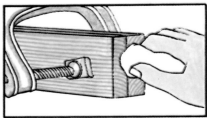

Spread the glue mixture on one surface and clamp the pieces together till dry. Wipe off excess glue straight away.

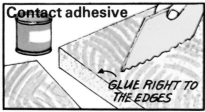

Contact adhesive

GLUE RIGHT TO THE EDGES

Use a contact adhesive such as "Evo-Stik" to stick plastic laminate to board. Spread glue on both surfaces to be joined.

Leave for 20 minutes, then press together. Make sure they are in the right position as this glue sticks instantly.

Resin glue

Resin glue, such as "Araldite" is two substances which you mix together. It sticks plastic and many other materials.

Spread the mixture on one of the surfaces to be joined, then fix in position till the glue is dry.

How to make a tool box

The easiest way to make a box with a lid is to make a solid box first, then saw across it to make the lid. For best results, make sure you saw the wood square to its edges.

Clamp the ends while you glue and hammer on the sides.

Then glue and nail on the top and base.

Draw two lines 5mm apart where you want the lid.

Saw across the box between the lines.

Then smooth back to the lines with a plane.

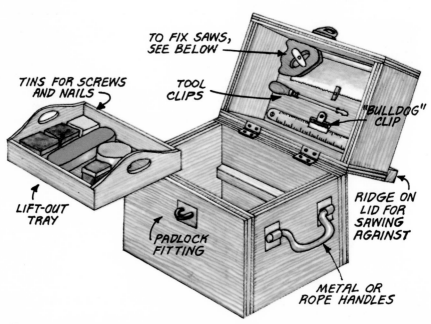

For saws, draw round the inside of the saw handle and cut this shape twice from thick softwood. Screw both pieces to the lid. Twist the top one over the handle to hold it in place.

Buying tools and equipment

With a tool kit like this you could tackle almost any woodwork job. There are plenty of things you can make, though, if you do not have all the tools shown here.

When you buy tools, remember that the more expensive ones are generally of a better quality than the cheaper ones, but they are made for craftsmen who use them everyday and expect them to last several years. You may not need to spend so much on your tools.

Saws

PANEL SAW

Panel saws are for thick wood or rough work.

TENON SAW

This is the most useful general purpose saw.

FRETSAW

COPING SAW

These are for sawing shapes. A coping saw is the more useful.

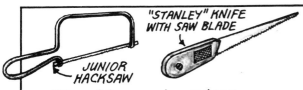

"STANLEY" KNIFE WITH SAW BLADE

JUNIOR HACKSAW

Either of these can be used as a cheaper substitute for a saw.

Care of saws

Lightly oil your saw when you put it away to stop it going rusty, and buy a saw-guard to protect the blade.

Hammers and mallets

You should use a hammer for hitting metal objects and a mallet for hitting wood. A hammer would bruise or split the wood. To keep your hammer head clean and smooth, rub it on fine glasspaper.

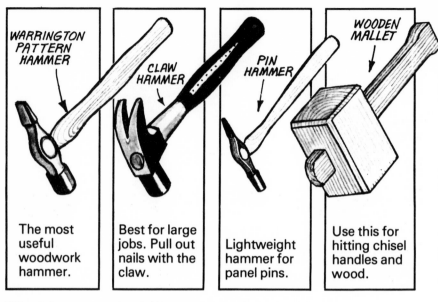

WARRINGTON PATTERN HAMMER

CLAW HAMMER

PIN HAMMER

WOODEN MALLET

The most useful woodwork hammer.

Best for large jobs. Pull out nails with the claw.

Lightweight hammer for panel pins.

Use this for hitting chisel handles and wood.

Marking out equipment

Make sure you have a good ruler and try square. The success of any project depends a lot on how accurate your measurements are.

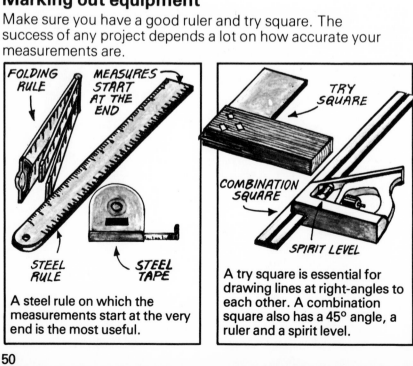

FOLDING RULE

MEASURES START AT THE END

STEEL RULE

STEEL TAPE

TRY SQUARE

COMBINATION SQUARE

SPIRIT LEVEL

A steel rule on which the measurements start at the very end is the most useful.

A try square is essential for drawing lines at right-angles to each other. A combination square also has a 45° angle, a ruler and a spirit level.

Sawing-boards

There are several different kinds of sawing-board. The most common is the standard sawing-board which you can buy or make for yourself, following the instructions on pages 17-18.

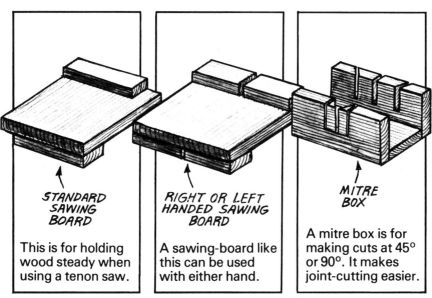

STANDARD SAWING BOARD

This is for holding wood steady when using a tenon saw.

RIGHT OR LEFT HANDED SAWING BOARD

A sawing-board like this can be used with either hand.

MITRE BOX

A mitre box is for making cuts at 45° or 90°. It makes joint-cutting easier.

Vices and clamps

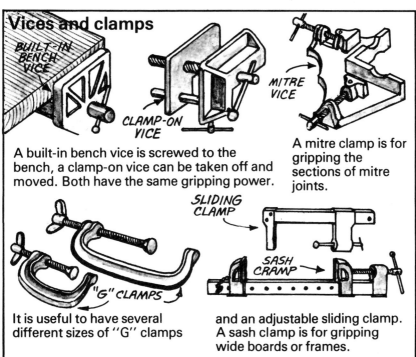

BUILT-IN BENCH VICE

CLAMP-ON VICE

MITRE VICE

A built-in bench vice is screwed to the bench, a clamp-on vice can be taken off and moved. Both have the same gripping power.

A mitre clamp is for gripping the sections of mitre joints.

SLIDING CLAMP

"G" CLAMPS

SASH CRAMP

It is useful to have several different sizes of "G" clamps

and an adjustable sliding clamp. A sash clamp is for gripping wide boards or frames.

Nails

When you buy nails you have to say what length and type of nail you want, e.g. "40mm oval brads". If you are not sure what to buy, ask the shop assistant for advice.

You can buy packets or boxes of different types of nails.

Large amounts are cheaper to buy by weight.

Types of nails

WIRE NAIL

Strong nails for rough woodwork.

LOST HEAD NAIL

Nails with small heads for punching into the wood.

OVAL BRAD

Nails with oval heads which are less likely to split the wood.

PANEL PIN

Fine nails for plywood, hardboard and small jobs.

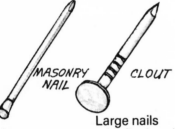

MASONRY NAIL   **CLOUT**

Very strong nails for bricks and walls.

Large nails with flat heads for felt or canvas.

CHAIR NAIL   **TACK**

Chair nails and tacks for nailing furniture covers and carpets.

STAPLE

"U" shaped nails for fixing wire to wood.

Lost head nails

NAIL PUNCH

Hammer the heads in with a nail punch.

Oval brads

GRAIN

Hammer these in with the oval shape along grain.

Wire nails

CLAW HAMMER

Wire nails have large heads, so are easy to pull out.

Screws

Screws are described by their length, size, type and the material they are made of.
The size is a number describing the width of the shank.
For example, "1in (25mm) No. 6 countersunk head steel screws".

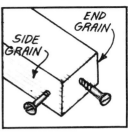

Screws grip better in the side grain than in the end grain.

Types of screws

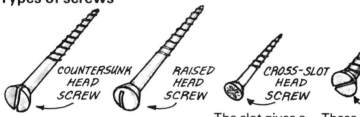

COUNTERSUNK HEAD SCREW

RAISED HEAD SCREW

CROSS-SLOT HEAD SCREW

CHIPBOARD SCREW

The head fits flat with the wood.

Only half the head fits into the wood.

The slot gives a good grip for the special screwdriver.

These have a long thread for extra gripping strength.

Screw caps

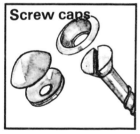

These are for covering up the heads of screws.

Screwdrivers

CROSS-SLOT SCREWDRIVER

Screwdrivers with blades 10mm wide and 5mm wide are useful, as well as a medium-sized cross-slot screwdriver.

Making pilot holes

BRADAWL

GIMLET

Fit screws into holes made by a gimlet, bradawl or drill.

Screws in thick wood

HOLE THE SIZE OF SCREW HEAD

DRILL BIT

Instead of buying long screws, you can drill counterbore holes, as shown in the picture, and set the screws into the wood.

Chisels

These are made in a number of different shapes and sizes. It is usually best to use the widest chisel possible for the job you are doing The most useful widths to buy are 6mm and 12mm.

The bevel-edged chisel reaches into corners and is a good, general purpose chisel. The firmer chisel is for heavier work.

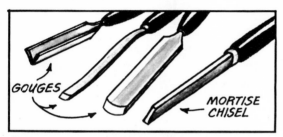

Gouges are a special kind of chisel for wood carving and the mortise chisel is for cutting the slots for joints called mortises.

Sharpening chisels

Chisels must be kept very sharp and a new chisel should be sharpened before you use it. You can find out how to sharpen a chisel on page 58.

Files and rasps

These are tools for shaping wood. The blades are sold separately from the handles and can be replaced. Rasps are rougher than files and quicker for removing large amounts of wood.

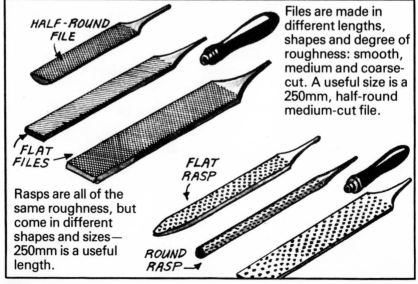

Files are made in different lengths, shapes and degree of roughness: smooth, medium and coarse-cut. A useful size is a 250mm, half-round medium-cut file.

Rasps are all of the same roughness, but come in different shapes and sizes— 250mm is a useful length.

Planes

A plane for smoothing wood to exact sizes is a useful but expensive piece of equipment. A cheaper substitute is the shaper plane shown below. Plane blades need to be kept very sharp – see page 58 for sharpening tools.

The jack plane and the smoothing plane are general purpose planes. The jack plane is larger and is more suitable for heavy work.

A block plane is for reaching into corners and other difficult places.

Shaper tools

These have blades with lots of little teeth like a cheese grater. They are made in various shapes for different jobs and can be used instead of planes, files or rasps.

These can be used instead of ordinary planes, but they do not produce quite such a smooth finish.

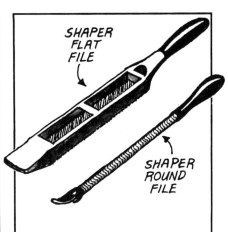

Shaper files do not clog up and the blades are cheap and easy to replace.

Drills

You need a drill to make holes for screws and dowels, and for making holes in which to put the blade of a coping saw when you want to saw a shape out of a piece of wood. The pieces that fit in the drill and make the holes are called "bits". Twist bits are for making ordinary holes and countersink bits are for making shallow holes for the heads of countersunk screws.

Hand drill

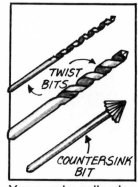

A hand drill can be used for making holes up to about 8mm in diameter. It is the most useful general purpose drill and takes twist or countersink bits.

You need a collection of several sizes of twist and countersink bits.

Carpenter's brace

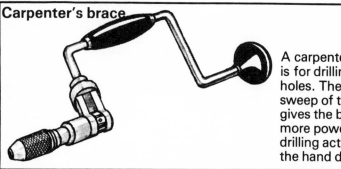

A carpenter's brace is for drilling large holes. The wide sweep of the handle gives the brace a more powerful drilling action than the hand drill.

Auger bit

SCREW TIP

This is the bit for a carpenter's brace. The screw tip helps pull the bit into the wood.

How to use a brace

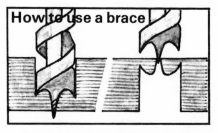

When the screw tip appears at the bottom, turn the wood and finish the hole from the other side.

Electric drill

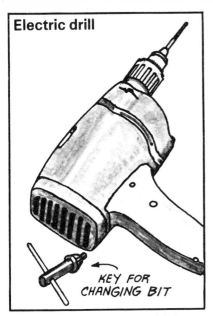

KEY FOR
CHANGING BIT

This is useful for drilling thick or hard materials. It takes twist and countersink bits, as well as special drill attachments.

Extras for an electric drill

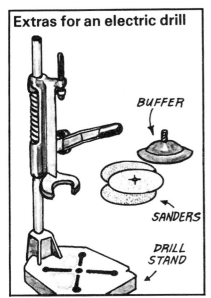

BUFFER

SANDERS

DRILL
STAND

Sanders and buffers are for smoothing and polishing wood. A drill stand holds the drill firmly for sanding, buffing and drilling.

How to use an electric drill

ON/OFF
SWITCH

Always hold the drill with both hands—one to support it and turn it on and off, and the other to direct it.

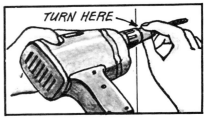

TURN HERE

Practice drilling some holes in scrap wood first. To start off, turn the drill by hand to make a guide mark.

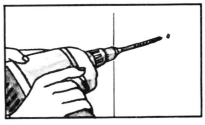

Drill a short way, then stop and check the hole is still in the right position before you continue.

Safety hints

★ Always put the electric flex over your shoulder to keep it out of the way.
★ Unplug the drill when you change the bit.
★ Make sure you are not standing on damp or wet ground.
★ Keep loose clothes, long hair or ties out of the way.

Sharpening tools

For best results you should always make sure your tools are sharp and in a good condition. You can sharpen chisel and plane blades yourself, but take your saw to a shop for sharpening.

A sharp chisel or plane blade should have two slopes. The first slope should be at an angle of 30° and the second at an angle of 25°.

Sharpen blades on an oilstone* wiped with fine machine oil.

To help you hold the blade at the correct angle while you sharpen it, a honing guide is useful.

Set the honing guide to 30° for a chisel or plane blade.

Put some oil on the oilstone then, with the blade in the honing guide, slide it backwards and forwards along the oilstone.

Keep checking the blade and stop when it gets rough on top.

Turn it over, hold it flat on the oilstone and rub it round and round to smooth off the roughness.

*An oilstone with two grades of hardness is the most useful.

Which wood or board?

The kind of wood you choose for a job depends on what it is for, whether it is for indoors or outside and how much you want to spend.

Instead of buying expensive hardwood, you can get plywood or chipboard with a thin cover, called a veneer, of hardwood. This is not suitable for outside though.

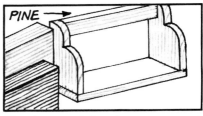

Pine is one of the cheaper natural woods. It varies in colour from cream to red and is suitable for most indoor jobs.

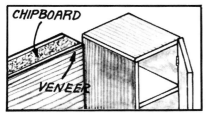

Veneered chipboard is good for shelves and cupboards, but you have to use special screws, hinges and other fittings.

Plywood comes in many different thicknesses. Use interior grade for indoors and exterior grade for outside.

Hardboard is useful for making flat, light covers for frames. It is available in various thicknesses.

Beech is very hardwearing and can be used for outdoors or for things which are not painted or varnished.

Oak is suitable for outdoors or indoors. Use brass, not steel screws with oak.

Lime is a softer hardwood than beech or oak and is good for carving.

First aid

When you are doing woodwork you will probably cut your fingers, bash your nails and get lots of splinters. You can deal with these yourself, but if a wound is serious call for help.

Small cuts

Wash the cut in cold water to clean it and stop the bleeding.

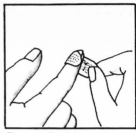

Dry well, then cover with sticky plaster to keep it clean.

Serious cuts

Press the wound hard with a clean handkerchief, tissue or your hands to reduce the bleeding.

Put the wound higher than the rest of your body to lessen the flow of blood. Find or call someone to help you.

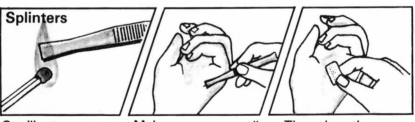

Splinters

Sterilize tweezers or a needle in the blue part of a flame.

Make sure you get all the splinter out.

Then clean the wound and cover it with sticky plaster.

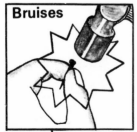

Bruises

Wash with cold water to reduce bruising and swelling.

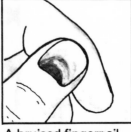

A bruised fingernail may go black. If very painful, see a doctor.

Blood blisters should be left to dry up, not popped.

Electric shocks

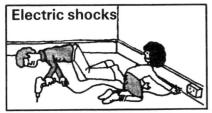

If someone has a bad electric shock, do not touch them. Try to switch off the electricity or pull out the plug.

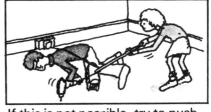

If this is not possible, try to push them away from the electricity. Use something made of wood which does not conduct the electricity to you.

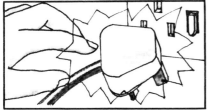

If you give yourself a slight electric shock you may feel weak, so relax a bit before carrying on working.

Look after someone who has hurt themselves badly. Keep them warm and get them to lie down while you call for help.

Safety hints

Many accidents can be avoided if you work carefully and think about what you are doing all the time. Always keep your tools tidy and out of other people's way.

Never hold the wood in your hand while you saw it.

Never screw into a piece of wood held in your hand.

Never chisel towards your hand.

Never chisel towards your body either.

Never use electric tools in damp or wet conditions.

Woodworking words

Bit
The piece that fits into a drill and makes the hole.

Counterboring
Drilling a hole the size of the head of a screw so it fits below the surface of the wood.

Countersinking
Drilling a shallow hole so the screw head lies flush with the surface of the wood.

Dimensions
The length, width and thickness of a piece of wood.

Dowels
Small rods of hardwood, often used like nails to join pieces of wood.

Finishing
The process of painting, varnishing, waxing or putting some other protective coating on wood.

Grain
The pattern of lines made by the fibres in the wood.

Hardwood
The kind of wood that comes from deciduous trees (trees that lose their leaves in the winter).

Joints
Ways of joining wood together—with nails, screws, dowels, or by cutting sections from pieces of wood so they fit together.

Man-made boards
Various kinds of board such as chipboard and plywood made in factories from natural wood.

Marking-out
Marking all the measurements for a project onto the wood.

Offcuts
Small pieces left after wood has been cut to size. Builders or woodshops usually sell them at a cheap price.

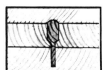

Pilot hole
A hole drilled the same size as a screw and into which the screw is fitted.

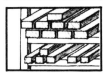

Pre-planed timber
Wood planed smooth before it is sold. It is measured before it is planed so it is always slightly smaller than its measurements.

Resizing
Accurately planing a piece of timber down to new dimensions.

Right-angle
An angle of 90°.

Sealing
Putting a coat of thinned varnish or paint on wood to make it smooth before painting, varnishing or waxing.

Shank
The smooth part of a screw, just below the head.

Softwood
The kind of wood that comes from coniferous trees (trees that do not lose their leaves in the winter).

Veneer
A thin layer of wood or plastic laminate covering cheaper wood or board.

Index